Under His Wings

Forgiveness

*Rejoicing in God's Forgiveness
and Living a Forgiven Life*

(A Study of Psalm 32)

Written by Martha Streufert Jander
Edited by Laine Rosin

CPH
Concordia Publishing House

Editorial assistant: Laura Christian

Copyright © 1999 by Concordia Publishing House
3558 South Jefferson Avenue, St. Louis, MO 63118-3968
Manufactured in the United States of America

This publication is also available in braille and in large print for the visually impaired. Write to Library for the Blind, 1333 S. Kirkwood Rd., St. Louis, MO 63122-7295; or call 1-800-433-3954.

Contents

David Rejoices in God's Forgiveness

Where Are We Going?

We will study David and how he rejoiced in the mercy and forgiveness that God gave him and how we are blessed with that same forgiveness.

Ready, Set, Go

Begin with prayer. Ask the Lord to bless your study of His Word and that He reveals Himself and His gracious love and forgiveness to you.

Spend a few minutes on "**Where Am I Now?**" to begin the discussion. Get into "**The Search**" to discover the blessings of forgiveness and the relief God gave to David when he repented of his sin and the relief He gives to us when we confess our sins.

Take time to "**Respond,**" reflecting on God's great love with praise and joy. Then pray together as a group.

Before the next session, do the "**Do,**" recording your thoughts and experiences in the journal page following this session, filling in the prayer page (or using it as a way to pray each day).

Where Am I Now?

Finish this sentence and discuss it with one or two partners: When I think of the term *being blessed,* I think of …

The Search
David's Confession

It appears that David may have written Psalm 32 some time after he confessed to God his sins of adultery and murder. The psalm is labeled "A Maskil," which many believe to mean a teaching psalm or one used for instruction. God exposed David's sin, conducted in what he surely hoped was in secret, not only to Israel but also for our learning. David had wrestled with his sin and felt the impact of its guilt, but he also experienced the gracious and loving hand of God's forgiving mercy. In the psalm David wanted his people as well to know the blessing of sin forgiven and joy restored. Read Psalm 32.

1. The New King James Version renders verses 1 and 2 in this way: "Blessed is he whose transgression is forgiven, whose sin is covered. Blessed is the man to whom the LORD does not impute iniquity, and in whose spirit there is no deceit." Underline or highlight here the four ways in which sin is identified and what God does about each.

2a. By the time God sent His prophet Nathan to confront David with his sin, Bathsheba was his wife and had borne their son. Read verses 3 and 4 of the psalm. What do these words say about David's state of mind since the time he had taken Bathsheba and had Uriah killed? What did David want the people of Israel to know about unrepented sin?

2b. What does God want us to know about unrepented sin? How has unrepented sin caused physical stress or anguish for you? What happens when we keep refusing to repent?

3a. Nathan's charge to David, "You are the man!" (2 Samuel 12:7), brought David up short. When accused, he had no choice but to admit his guilt. Read verses 5–7 of the psalm. What does David finally admit? What do these verses say about God? What do they indicate about David's belief in God?

3b. What brings you to repent? Describe the relief you experience when you confess your sins and hear the good news that you are forgiven because of Christ? How will God receive you?

David's Anguish

4a. Read 2 Samuel 12:15–25. What do David's prayer and mourning show about him? about his hope in God? Why did David stop mourning when his son died? Why do you suppose he went to the temple at that point to worship?

4b. How do you mourn over your sin and its consequences? How do you rejoice when you hear (or remember or read) the words that God forgives your sin and cleanses you from your unrighteousness?

David's Blessedness

5. God forgave David and gave to him and Bathsheba another son, Solomon, which may be derived from the Hebrew for "peace." Through Nathan the prophet God chose another name for him, Jedidiah, meaning "loved by the Lord." Why are these two names appropriate? What do they say of David's relationship with God?

6a. Read verses 8–11 of the psalm. What does David want the people (and us) to learn from his experience? How does David respond here to God's forgiving love? How does he want the people to respond?

6b. What do these words mean for you? Write any words of a psalm or hymn that come to mind as you reflect on God's grace and unending mercy to you. Be ready to share these words under "Respond."

Respond

Ponder in silence for several minutes God's great love. Then share in your small group or with the entire group your answer to 6b.

Sing a hymn or use the words of Psalm 32:10b–11 to speak God's praise together. Close with a group prayer, bringing to God any concerns mentioned during today's study.

Do

This week ask God to make you truly repentant as you lay your sins before Him. He washes them away and renews your heart and life. His grace is yours through the Gospel and the Sacraments. Record your thoughts on the journal page.

Additional Bible readings for this week: Psalm 40; Jeremiah 31:31–34; and Mark 2:1–12. Copy and attach to a mirror or other place you see daily the words of Jeremiah 31:34c.

Use the prayer starters each day as you come to the Lord, either writing in your own endings to the sentences or leaving them blank to be used in a new way each day.

For next week, read about Mary Magdalene in Mark 15:40–41; 16:9; Luke 8:1–3; and John 20:10–18. Read through Session 2, filling in any responses as you like.

Journal Page

O Lord, You are so _____

_____

_____

_____

and I am so _____

_____

_____

_____

Please forgive me for _____

_____

_____

_____

_____

Help me _____

_____

_____

_____

_____

Please bless and take care of _____

_____

_____

_____

_____

Thanks, Lord, for _____

_____

_____

_____

_____

Session 2

Jesus Forgives Mary Magdalene

Where Are We Going?

We will discover how Mary Magdalene, empowered by God's forgiveness of her sins through Jesus, and filled by the Spirit with love, spent her life serving Jesus and ministering to His needs. We will see how God empowers us with forgiveness and fills us with His Spirit so that we too can serve.

Ready, Set, Go

Begin with prayer. Ask the Lord to free you for service to Him and to others.

Spend a few minutes on **"Where Am I Now?"** as you begin the study. Get into **"The Search"** to discover where true freedom, joy, and the power for service are found.

Take time to **"Respond,"** to thank and praise God for the robe of righteousness that you now wear. Then pray together, asking God to help you realize that forgiveness is yours in Jesus.

Before the next session, do the **"Do,"** recording your thoughts and experiences in the journal page and filling in the prayer page.

Where Am I Now?

Describe a favorite dress or outfit that you had as a child or teenager (or even more recently). What made it special?

The Search

Mary Magdalene, the Sinner

Not many verses in the Bible are devoted to information about Mary Magdalene. We do learn that she was from the city of Magdala, a city in Galilee along the western coast of the Sea of Galilee, not more than 10 miles from Capernaum. Mark and Luke tell us that Mary had been possessed by seven demons, from which Jesus had freed her. Demon-possession tormented people to the point of destruction of body and soul. Read Mark 16:9.

1a. Seven is the biblical number for completion, and Mary Magdalene was possessed by seven demons. This might indicate that she was completely possessed when Jesus healed her. While we don't know what specific sins these demons dragged Mary into, they undoubtedly dominated her life for a time. Look up some of the following verses and record the damage demons inflicted on the people they possessed: Matthew 9:32; 17:15; Mark 5:2–5; and Luke 9:38–42.

1b. Discuss how people today get pulled into the occult or begin to worship the devil. Just as Satan promised good to Eve but delivered evil, what ploys does he take to draw people into his web of deceit today? What physical or emotional damage can result?

1c. Many times "little" sins seem to possess us, chaining us to actions or habits we abhor but can't throw off. We may even stop fighting them. What might these sins be that you or someone you know struggle with?

What can be the consequences of those sins? of ignoring those sins?

Sometimes Satan's attacks on us are more than a constant or persistent pecking—they become outright vicious attacks. Perhaps you or someone you know suffers from extreme anxiety and cannot know the joy of true forgiveness because Satan keeps you or them enshrouded with storm clouds of guilt. One might experience abnormal fear or torment about never being good enough. These demons keep attacking because they want to draw us away from Jesus and the peace and joy He offers.

2. Stop at this time and ask the Lord to deliver you or others you know from Satan's grip. By His death and resurrection Jesus has defeated Satan. He comes to us in Word and Sacraments with power to break those bonds that still seek to ensnare us; indeed He has broken them by His death and glorious resurrection. Write down some of the promises God has given to you.

Mary Magdalene, the Servant

3a. When Jesus heals, it is always complete. The demons left Mary entirely, and her life changed. She, along with a number of other women, used her time and resources to minister to Jesus and His disciples. Read Luke 8:1–3 and Mark 15:40–41. How did Mary demonstrate her gratefulness to Jesus and the peace and joy He gave? Why do you think this was important to Mary?

14

3b. Jesus' forgiveness for you is complete. How is your life different from what it was or would be if you didn't know Jesus? From what has Jesus freed you? How can you show your joy in the freedom of love and forgiveness that Jesus gives you?

Mary Magdalene, the Blessed

4a. Mary Magdalene was one of the women who stood by and watched Jesus die and then looked on as He was buried. Read Mark 15:40–41, 47. Describe what Mary might have been going through as she observed her Lord's death and burial. What thoughts might have been going through her mind? What did Mary not understand at that time?

4b. We see from this side of Easter that in order for Mary Magdalene, the other women, the disciples, and all people to be truly forgiven, Jesus had to die. God's wrath had to be appeased, His justice satisfied. On Jesus God laid all our sin—its guilt and its punishment, complete and final. What does this mean for you?

5a. Read John 20:1–18. How does this confirm Jesus' love and forgiveness for Mary? In what ways did

Jesus bless Mary? How does this incident depict Mary's love for Jesus?

5b. Jesus promises that He is present in Word and Sacraments. In what ways does He bless you? Recall times when you were blessed by Jesus' love and forgiveness through these means of grace.

6a. Look at Psalm 32. With which verses might Mary Magdalene identify? Why might verses 7, 10, and 11 have special meaning for her? In what could Mary surely rest secure? What could Mary teach or instruct you about the way you should go (verse 8)?

6b. Copy a verse or two from the psalm that speak of God's forgiveness to you. Why can you rely on these words of God? How could you teach or instruct someone concerning God's forgiveness?

Respond

Jesus clothes us with the robe of His righteousness. We cannot—no, dare not—appear before God wearing even our very best outfit. Jesus' death and resurrection was enough to cover us perfectly. Sing or say together the following song:

Jesus, Your blood and righteousness
My beauty are, my glorious dress;
Mid flaming worlds, in these arrayed,
With joy shall I lift up my head.

Bold shall I stand in that great day,
Cleansed and redeemed, no debt to pay;
For by Your cross absolved I am
From sin and guilt, from fear and shame.

Pray together, thanking God for His love and mercy, given you in Jesus, your Savior.

Do

This week be aware of times when Satan's attacks are evident. Be prepared to fight him with the Word of God. Write in your journal, "Go away, Satan. Do not bother me! I am a child of God, and He protects me from you."

Additional Bible readings: Psalm 130; Mark 2:1–12; and Revelation 12:7–12. Copy and attach to a place you see daily the verse from Psalm 32 that you recorded in question 6b.

Write in your own endings to the prayer starters or leave them blank to be used in a new way each day.

For next week, read in Luke 7:36–50 about the woman who washed Jesus' feet. Read through Session 3, filling in any responses as you like.

Journal Page

_____
_____
_____
_____
_____
_____
_____
_____
_____
_____
_____
_____
_____
_____
_____
_____
_____
_____
_____
_____
_____
_____
_____
_____
_____
_____
_____
_____
_____
_____

O Lord, You are so _____

_____

_____

_____

and I am so _____

_____

_____

_____

Please forgive me for _____

_____

_____

_____

_____

Help me _____

_____

_____

_____

_____

Please bless and take care of _____

_____

_____

_____

_____

Thanks, Lord, for _____

_____

_____

_____

_____

The Woman Who Washed Jesus' Feet

Where Are We Going?

We will discover the depth of love Jesus had for the forgiven woman and for us and the love the woman had for Jesus; we will discuss how we can respond with the same love in our daily lives.

Ready, Set, Go

Begin with prayer. Ask the Lord to bless this study of His Word as you discover the power of His love and what it can mean for your life.

Spend just a few minutes on **"Where Am I Now?"** Get into **"The Search"** to keep God's promise of forgiveness and the power of His love ever before you.

Take time to **"Respond"** with words of forgiveness and pardon. Then pray as a group, bringing your concerns to the Lord's throne.

Before the next session, do the **"Do."** Record your thoughts and experiences in the journal page and fill in the prayer page.

Where Am I Now?

What is the most outrageous thing that a guest might do (or has done) at a gathering you host (or have hosted)? What would your reaction be? How would your other guests react?

The Search

The Setting

This story is told early in the Gospel of Luke (chapter 7) and most likely took place during the spring of the second year of our Lord's ministry. The event is often confused with Mary of Bethany's anointing of Jesus, which took place during Holy Week, just before Jesus' crucifixion. Luke refers to the woman in chapter 7 as "a woman who had lived a sinful life" (verse 37), never giving her name. The belief that this was Mary Magdalene has been argued but most often disproved by biblical scholars. We are told only that this woman was a sinner, a harlot with a bad reputation. Read Luke 7:36–39 to see what this sinful woman did for Jesus and how the host reacted.

1a. What compelled the woman to act as she did? What do her actions say about her and what she knew about Jesus? What did Jesus know about her?

1b. How would you react to a derelict walking into your worship service and sitting in the front pew? to a beggar stumbling into your garden party to ask for handouts?

1c. What does Jesus know about you? What do you know about Jesus? How do your actions reflect your relationship with Him?

2. Why do you think the woman wasn't concerned about the other people present, especially the Pharisee and his cohorts?

The Lesson

The Pharisees of Jesus' day and those who followed them lived by the letter of the Law. They believed that they could gain God's favor and heaven by keeping outwardly clean and doing all that the Law required. They even added more rules and regulations when they thought God's Word was insufficient, making their interpretations and traditions part of the law. The Pharisees regularly sought Jesus out—not to listen and learn but to find fault and ask questions they hoped would entrap Jesus. Most often they were left stammering for answers to questions Jesus asked them. Read Jesus' response to the Pharisee's thoughts about the sinful woman in Luke 7:40–50.

3a. How did Simon react when Jesus asked him about the two debtors? Why do you think Jesus used this story to bring home His point about forgiveness? Make two lists, one showing what Simon did for Jesus, the other what the woman did.

3b. How do you react to Jesus when He says to you, "Your sins are forgiven"? List what you have done to show your love for Jesus in the past week.

The Message

Jesus tried to impress on Simon the fact that this woman, though a sinner, was penitent and forgiven. He wanted the Pharisee to know that she showed love to Him not in order to be forgiven, but because she had been forgiven. "We love because He first loved us" (1 John 4:19). God's love flows from us to others. Water is poured onto a plant, which lives and grows and produces blossoms. So we, as forgiven Christians into whom God pours His love, live in Him, grow in grace and mercy to others, and produce the good fruits of righteousness.

4a. Discuss other biblical people who showed love to Jesus because they were forgiven. How did they show that love?

4b. How do you show love to Jesus because you are forgiven? What do you do for others to reflect the love God has abundantly poured on you?

5a. Another product of God's forgiveness and mercy to us is our ability and willingness to forgive others. Why is this sometimes hard to do? Why does Jesus stress the importance of forgiving others (see Matthew 18:21–35; Mark 11:24–25; and Colossians 3:13)? What might the unwillingness to forgive indicate?

5b. How can we become willing and able to forgive others (see Romans 7:6; 8:26–28; and Colossians 3:16–17)?

6a. "As far as the east is from the west, so far has He removed our transgressions from us" (Psalm 103:12). Not only has He forgiven us, but God also says, "I will forgive their wickedness and will remember their sins no more" (Jeremiah 31:34). Why is it also important for us to view those sins as forgiven?

6b. Are there grudges that you harbor in your heart or people you refuse to forgive because it would be "condoning" their actions? Read Psalm 32. The results that David describes concerning an impenitent heart could very well describe the unforgiving heart. When we refuse to forgive, then there is doubt about true penitence over our own sins. In silence during the next few minutes, go to your Father in heaven. Ask Him to turn you to Him in true repentance, to make you willing and able to forgive others as He has forgiven you. Record some key words. God is faithful and will do what He has promised.

Respond

Are there sins you carry with you because you can't believe you are forgiven? God does not lie or give false hope. He is true to His many promises to forgive. He will never retract or retreat.

Pair up with one or two other people. Confess your sins with these words: "I am a poor sinner. I have not trusted God or loved my neighbor as I should." Declare to each other, "God has forgiven you for the sake of Jesus, His Son. He has removed your sins from you as far as the east is from the west. Go in peace."

Pray together in your large group, asking God for His boundless love and precious forgiveness through Jesus.

Do

This week be aware of times when you hold onto grudges or are unforgiving toward someone. Record these times in your journal, ask the Lord to give you a forgiving heart, then record how the Lord responded.

Additional Bible readings for this week: Matthew 18:21–35; Luke 23:26–49; and Romans 8:1–17. Copy and attach to a mirror or other place you see daily the words of Luke 7:50.

Use the prayer starters each day. Write in your own endings or leave them blank to be used in a new way each day.

For next week, reread Psalm 32. Read through Session 4, filling in any responses as you like.

Journal Page

_____
_____
_____
_____
_____
_____
_____
_____
_____
_____
_____
_____
_____
_____
_____
_____
_____
_____
_____
_____
_____
_____
_____
_____
_____
_____
_____
_____
_____
_____

O Lord, You are so _____

_____

_____

_____

and I am so _____

_____

_____

_____

Please forgive me for _____

_____

_____

_____

Help me _____

_____

_____

_____

Please bless and take care of _____

_____

_____

_____

Thanks, Lord, for _____

_____

_____

_____

Session 4
Easter People

Where Are We Going?

We will look at the joy that is ours through God's forgiving love to us in Jesus and take a more intense look at Psalm 32.

Ready, Set, Go

Begin with prayer. Ask the Lord to bless your study of His Word with the power and joy of the Spirit.

Spend a few minutes on "**Where Am I Now?**" to get into the study. Spend the major portion of your time on "**The Search**" and look at Psalm 32 in reflection of God's forgiving love.

You may want to spend a few minutes extra on "**Respond**," as you write your own psalm. Then use your psalm as a closing prayer in the larger group.

Do the "**Do**," recording your thoughts and experiences in the journal page following this session, filling in the prayer page (or using it as a way to pray each day).

Where Am I Now?

What are you always ready to do either by yourself or with family or friends?

Forgiveness

1. In the space below, write your definition of forgiveness.

2a. Read Psalm 32:1–7. How does David describe himself as an impenitent sinner? What is God's definition of forgiveness as revealed through David?

2b. How would you describe your experience when sin has laid heavy upon you?

3. List what the mighty waters were for David mentioned in verse 6 of the psalm, for Mary Magdalene, and for the sinful woman.

4a. Draw a picture of a hiding place or use descriptive words to tell about it. How can this be your picture of God's rescue of you? Why is knowing God in this way important?

4b. How might Mary Magdalene and the sinful woman describe God's hiding place for them?

Read verses 8–11 of the psalm. God wants us to know that He always pardons our sin because of Jesus' death on the cross. Therefore, He wants us to turn to Him in repentance, and He promises to forgive. When He forgives, He does not leave us alone to find our own way or stumble along, but He stays with us to guide us and show us the way He would have us live. However, some scholars believe that in verses 8–9 David is talking to others so that they will not follow foolish ways but will instead return to the Lord.

5a. What would Mary Magdalene and the sinful woman want others to know about Jesus and His forgiving love?

5b. What do you want to teach others about God's forgiving love?

6a. As you look at verse 9, discuss the difference between a mule or horse that needs a bridle and bit and a Christian living in God's realm of grace.

6b. How did David, Mary Magdalene, and the sinful woman reflect that Christian living? What did God's forgiveness enable them to do?

6c. What does God's forgiveness enable you to do? How does your life reflect that? How can your relationship to God grow because of His love for you? How can your relationship with others improve because He has forgiven you?

7. Record your reflection of the term "Easter people." What does that mean for you? What joy is yours because of who you are and what God has made you in Christ?

Respond

God's redemption for us in Jesus turns our lives around, gives joy where there is sorrow, hope where there is despair. It tears down walls of distrust and disdain and bridges the gaps grudges and an unwilling spirit have made in our lives. Because of Christ we are transformed into joy-filled, forgiving, encouraging Easter people of God.

Use the space below to write your own psalm of thanksgiving and praise to God for His forgiving love.

Use your psalm or a section of it as your part in the group prayer, adding any other needs or concerns.

Do

This week thank God several times a day for His forgiving love for you. Ask for His Spirit to give you a willing, forgiving, Easter heart filled with His joy and love. Record those times in your journal.

Additional Bible readings for this week: Psalms 81 and 98; Matthew 28:1–10; and Philippians 4. Copy and attach to a mirror or other place you see daily the words of Philippians 4:7.

Use the prayer starters each day as you come to the Lord, either writing in your own endings to the sentences or leaving them blank to be used in a new way each day.

Continue your daily Bible reading and prayer. Use a journal to record your faith journey. If you are continuing with another study, read through the first session.

Journal Page

O Lord, You are so _____

_____

_____

_____

and I am so _____

_____

_____

_____

Please forgive me for _____

_____

_____

_____

_____

Help me _____

_____

_____

_____

_____

Please bless and take care of _____

_____

_____

_____

_____

Thanks, Lord, for _____

_____

_____

_____

_____

O Lord, You are so

and I am so

Please forgive me for

Help me

Please bless and take care of

Thanks, Lord, for

Under His Wings

Guilt

Looking to God
in Times of Guilt and Confession

(A Study of Psalms 38 and 51)

Written by Martha Streufert Jander
Edited by Laine Rosin

CPH
Concordia Publishing House

Editorial assistant: Laura Christian

Contents

Eve: First Woman, First Sinner

Where Are We Going?

We will study Eve, mother of all the living, who listened to temptation and found it appealing; we will look at ourselves and discover what makes sin appealing to us; we will confess our sins using Psalms 38 and 51.

Ready, Set, Go

Begin with prayer. Ask God to open your eyes to see the reality of the consequences of sin and to turn you away from sin and toward Him and His grace.

Spend a few minutes on "**Where Am I Now?**" Circle definitions and discuss how we at times minimize or excuse sin. Get into "**The Search**" to discover how God views sin and what the consequences of sin brought to a perfect world.

Take time to "**Respond**," confessing your sin to one another, then gathering as a group to pray together and thank God for His mercy and forgiveness.

Before the next session, do the "**Do**," recording your thoughts and experiences in the journal page following this session and filling in the prayer page (or using it as a way to pray each day).

Where Am I Now?

Circle and add your own words frequently used as a substitute for the word *sin*. Briefly discuss how people minimize or excuse sin.

mistake   wrong   blunder   error   fumble   flaw
depravity   transgression   slip   lapse   backslide
whoops!

The Temptation

1. Eve was innocent, beautiful, virtuous, and perfect not only in body but in soul and spirit as well, created in the likeness of God: "So God created man in His own image, in the image of God He created him; male and female He created them" (Genesis 1:27). Describe in your own words the phrase "in the image of God." Then describe the position Eve held at the time of her creation.

God had set a tree in the middle of the garden—the tree of the knowledge of good and evil. And God told Adam and Eve that they might eat of every other tree in the garden, but of that tree, they should not eat. Martin Luther suggests that Adam and Eve's obedience to God's command was in essence their worship of Him. But their paradise was not to last. Read Genesis 3:1–7 to see what happened to change things, not only for Adam and Eve, but for the whole course of humankind and the rest of creation.

2a. Read verse 1 again. How did the devil twist God's words as he spoke to Eve? What advantages did he promise? What was his goal? When did Eve make her first mistake? How did her reply (verses 2–3) show that she was still determined to trust God?

2b. Satan has not changed his ways. He still perverts God's Word and its meaning. Discuss how Satan warps God's Word today for people, for you. For what purpose does Satan do this?

3a. Look at verses 4–8. What do these verses reveal about sin? about temptation? about the results of sin?

3b. How were Eve's eyes indeed "opened"? How were her eyes opened to what Satan really was? How did Paradise, the Garden of Eden, suddenly change for Eve? How did she change?

3c. How have your eyes been opened as a result of your own sin or of someone's sin against you? How has Satan deceived you or someone you know? How have your circumstances changed as a result of sin? How were you changed?

4a. Read verses 9–13. If God is all-knowing and all-seeing, why do you suppose He asked, "Where are you?" Why did Adam and Eve respond the way they did? How did Adam even manage to lay some of the blame on God?

4b. Where in the Bible does God confront you with your sin?

5a. Read Psalm 38. What words might especially describe what Eve was experiencing at this time?

5b. What words from the psalm would you choose to describe your experiences with the aftermath of sin? How would you describe the situation in your own words?

The Sentencing

6a. Read Genesis 3:14–24. What is your response to God's sentencing of Eve? How had what God had meant as joy now become a burden and sorrow? How is mercy mixed with God's judgment?

6b. What is your response to God's promise in Genesis 3:15? How did God fulfill that promise? What means did He take to assure that Adam and Eve could not bring total destruction on themselves?

6c. What does God's promise mean for you?

Respond

God lifted the ultimate punishment for sin from the backs of Adam and Eve and took it upon Himself. "But He was wounded for our transgressions, He was bruised for our iniquities; the chastisement for our peace was upon Him, and by His stripes we are healed" (Isaiah 53:5 NKJV). Through Jesus Christ, His only Son, God made whole again the broken relationship that Adam and Eve had caused. Jesus, through His death and resurrection, made whole the broken relationship you were born into.

Choose two or three verses from Psalm 51 as a way of confessing your sins to one another. Do so in groups of two or three. Then speak the words of 1 John 2:12 (NKJV) to each other: "Your sins are forgiven you for His name's sake."

Pray together as a large group, thanking God for the forgiveness that is yours in Christ Jesus, acknowledging that He has indeed forgiven you and removed the guilt of your sins.

Do

This week be aware of times when you feel the burden of your sins. Record those in your journal. Borrow words from Psalm 38 or 51 or use your own words to describe your hopelessness or guilt. Then record the words that Jesus spoke to the paralytic in Luke 5:20, "Friend, your sins are forgiven."

Additional Bible readings for this week: Psalm 25; Luke 5:17–26; and 1 John 1:1–2:2. Copy and attach to a mirror or other place you see daily the last part of Hebrews 8:12.

Use the prayer starters each day as you come to the Lord in your quiet time, either writing in your own endings to the sentences or leaving them blank to be used in a new way each day.

Before the next session, read about Miriam in Numbers 12:1–16. Read through Session 2, filling in any responses as you like.

Journal Page

O Lord, You are so _____

_____

_____

_____

and I am so _____

_____

_____

Please forgive me for _____

_____

_____

_____

_____

Help me _____

_____

_____

_____

Please bless and take care of _____

_____

_____

_____

_____

Thanks, Lord, for _____

_____

_____

_____

_____

Session 2
Miriam: Rebellion

Where Are We Going?

We will see how Miriam rebelled against Moses and against God, setting herself in opposition to God's plans; we will see how God brought her back to Himself in repentance. We will also look at how we oppose God's plans for us and the consequences that can result and how God in Jesus brings us back to Himself in love.

Ready, Set, Go

Begin with prayer. Ask God to help you see the rebellion against Him in your own heart and His plan for you. Ask Him to turn you back to Him with His love and mercy.

Spend a few minutes on **"Where Am I Now?"** Talk about any rebellions you may have had as a teenager. Get into **"The Search,"** seeing how God holds on to Miriam and to us in our sinfulness, using different ways of bringing us back to Him.

Take time to **"Respond,"** letting the wonder of God's love for you in Jesus wash over you and refresh you. Then pray together, bringing your needs before God's throne of grace.

Before the next session, do the **"Do,"** recording your thoughts and experiences in the journal page and filling in the prayer page (or using it as a way to pray each day).

Where Am I Now?

Think back to your days as a teenager. What were some things you or teenagers in general rebelled against? Why? What were the results of your rebellion?

The Search

The Situation

Under the leadership of Moses, the children of Israel had left Egypt and were in their second year of traveling toward the Promised Land. God had given them the Ten Commandments at Mount Sinai, but they had not yet had reports on the land they were to claim. Just before this chapter is the account of God feeding and filling the people with manna and quail and also of God appointing the 70 elders to help Moses in governing His people.

1a. Now Miriam, perhaps the instigator since she is mentioned first, and Aaron find fault with Moses. Read Numbers 12:1–10a. What were their complaints? How did God respond?

1b. What was Miriam's sin? Why was God so angry?

1c. Read the following: Exodus 15:11; Isaiah 29:23; 64:6; Lamentations 4:13–16; and Matthew 5:48. What do these verses tell you about God? about us and our relationship to God? What does God demand from us? How do you respond to God's demand?

2a. Why do you suppose Moses didn't speak up for himself? Why did God take up his cause?

2b. What unjust criticisms are sometimes leveled at church leaders today? How do they react? How does the church react? How can you encourage and support your church leaders?

2c. Have you ever been the victim or perpetrator of unjust criticism? How did you (or the one you criti cized) react? What was the outcome of the criticism?

God's Sentence

3a. Read Numbers 12:10–16. We might think that God was unduly harsh with Miriam while Aaron got away with his sin. But because Miriam seems to be the instigator here and Aaron the follower, God seems to want us to know the difference between those who lead into sin and those who are misled. What would Aaron's role, as priest, be toward Miriam, who now had leprosy? Why did Aaron react to seeing Miriam as he did?

3b. What is the difference between the consequences of sin and the punishment for sin? Give examples. Why might we suffer the consequences of sin but never the punishment? Why does God allow us to suffer the consequences of sin—ours and others?

4a. A further consequence of Miriam's and Aaron's sin came when the whole company of Israel had to stop its journey for the seven days Miriam was put out of the camp. In a way, this was a rebuke to the people, who themselves had murmured against Moses. At the same time, how did this action show God's grace and love toward Miriam?

4b. How has God given you His grace and love at the same time that He shows you—or allows you to experience—the consequences of your sin? How does God want us to treat those who sin?

5a. Describe what you think Aaron experienced when he had to turn to Moses—whom he had just criticized—for help. What do you think was going through Miriam's mind at this time?

5b. What do you experience when you have to ask for help from someone in your family (a coworker, a stranger, a fellow church member) whom you have criticized?

God's Grace

6a. God's love is never-ending. He might seem to turn His back on us for a while to let us see how devastating sin and its consequences can be. But He always welcomes repentant sinners with the open arms and nail-pierced hands of Jesus. Read Psalm 38 as you think Miriam might have read it. With which verses might Miriam especially have identified? How could Miriam be assured of God's continuing love and forgiveness? (See Micah 6:4.)

6b. Which words in Psalm 38 could you use as confession and contrition? Which words speak especially of God's love and mercy to you?

Respond

We may not always understand the why or how of God's actions, but we can know that He loves us perfectly. Our love for Him should permeate all that we do and every other relationship that we have. God also knows that we are weak sinful beings. That is why His plan of salvation is so amazing. He loves us so much that He sent His Son to become one of us, to experience the same temptations that we do, but without sinning. He sent His Son to suffer the punishment that rightly belonged to us. And God sends His Holy Spirit who works through God's Word of Law to show us our sin and to bring us to repentance. The Holy Spirit works in Baptism, preaching, Absolution, and the Lord's Supper to deliver God's forgiveness. As a result, we are enabled to lead God-pleasing lives.

Read Psalm 51 together. Know that your sins are washed away by the blood of your Savior.

Pray together. Thank God for His love and mercy to you in Jesus Christ.

Do

This week be aware of times when you are tempted to be critical of others. Ask God to give you the understanding and love of Jesus for those with whom you interact. Use your journal page to record the love and forgiveness you experience from God's hand, given freely in Baptism, Absolution, the Lord's Supper, and in the Gospel message.

Additional Bible readings for this week: Luke 23:32–47; Romans 5:1–11; and Romans 6. Copy and attach to a mirror or other place you see daily the words of Romans 5:8.

Use the prayer starters each day as you come to the Lord in your quiet time, either writing in your own endings to the sentences or leaving them blank to be used in a new way each day.

For next week, read about David in 2 Samuel 11:1–12:12. Read Session 3, filling in responses as you like.

Journal Page

_____
_____
_____
_____
_____
_____
_____
_____
_____
_____
_____
_____
_____
_____
_____
_____
_____
_____
_____
_____
_____
_____
_____
_____
_____
_____
_____
_____

O Lord, You are so _____

and I am so _____

Please forgive me for _____

Help me _____

Please bless and take care of _____

Thanks, Lord, for _____

Session 3

David: Guilty As Charged

Where Are We Going?

We will see how God convicted David of his sin and then covered David with His forgiveness and grace; we will see how God convicts us of our sin and then covers us with His forgiveness and grace, gained for us by Jesus' death on the cross.

Ready, Set, Go

Begin with prayer. Turn yourself over to God. Ask the Lord to reveal your sins to you so that you might come to Him in contrition and repentance, knowing that, for Jesus' sake, He forgives you.

Spend a few minutes on **"Where Am I Now?"** Discuss briefly what happens when public officials sin. Get into **"The Search"** to expand your knowledge of sin and its consequences and of God's mercy and grace on behalf of all sinners.

Take time to **"Respond,"** remembering what God has done for you in Christ Jesus.

Before the next session, do the **"Do,"** recording your thoughts and experiences in the journal page and filling in the prayer page (or using it as a way to pray each day).

Where Am I Now?

Briefly discuss this question: Should public officials be accountable for their private actions to those who elect them? Why or why not?

The Search

The Opportunity

David, a king after God's own heart, fell to temptation and sinned against God, against his own flesh, against Bathsheba, against Uriah, and against the people of Israel.

David had been king of Israel for about 20 years at this time. He had won many victories over Israel's enemies and was acclaimed by all as a hero. Now the armies of Israel were fighting the Ammonites, their ancient enemies. David's rightful place should have been with his troops. Instead, he sent Joab out with the army and neglected his responsibility as head of the forces. Read of David's temptation and fall into sin in 2 Samuel 11:1–27.

1a. What does this story tell you about David? about Bathsheba? about Uriah? Why do you suppose God wanted this particular story included in Scripture?

1b. What temptations do you face? What circumstances can make temptations have stronger influence or be more appealing?

2a. Why do you think Bathsheba gave in to King David so easily? What might have influenced her? What might have fooled her? What reason or excuse might she have used in going to the king's house? What reasons might she have given for refusing?

2b. What influences surround us on a daily basis and tempt us to sin? What excuses do we use when we fall?

The Tangled Web

3. How and why did David use his power to try to influence Uriah? How does Uriah confound David's plan? Why do you think David responded the way he did?

The Accusation

4a. Read 2 Samuel 12:1–12. What is God's response to David's sin?

4b. Sin may be fun while we're doing it or we may think, It's such a little thing; it doesn't matter, or even, Who's going to know? But, as Nathan told David, "Why did you despise the word of the LORD by doing what is evil in His eyes?" (verse 9). God demands of us: "Be holy because I, the LORD your God, am holy" (Leviticus 19:2); and Jesus says, "Be perfect, therefore, as your heavenly Father is perfect" (Matthew 5:48). If God is holy, what must His response be to our sin? to all sin? Why is it important to know this? How do we despise the Word of the Lord when we deliberately go our own way?

What is your personal response to God's demand to be perfect?

The Confession and Forgiveness

5a. Read 2 Samuel 12:13, then read Psalm 38, a confession of sin written by David though the *specific* situation is not identified. How does this psalm describe David's situation? What word pictures does David use to express his burden of sin and guilt?

5b. Record in your own words the burden of guilt you experience when your own sin overwhelms you. Borrow words from David if you like.

6a. Now read Psalm 51, David's confession to God. What words tell of David's trust in God's forgiveness and his reliance on God's faithfulness?

6b. In what do you place your confidence that God forgives you? How are the benefits of Christ's sacrificial death now yours?

Respond

When we know Jesus, we know the Father (John 14:6–21), who gave His only Son into death for our sins, that we might be made right and holy in His sight. Because of Jesus' death and resurrection, we no longer have to hide our face in shame and misery. God has taken Jesus' robe of righteousness and covered us and our sin with His holiness. His death becomes our death; His holiness becomes our holiness; His resurrection becomes our resurrection.

Read Psalm 51 together or take turns reading it verse by verse. Highlight or underline words that stand out for you. Share the words you marked. If you like, tell why they have special meaning.

Pray together, confessing your sins to God the Father. God hears and forgives you for the sake of Jesus, His Son. Praise God for His great love and mercy.

Do

This week ask God to make you more aware of times when you are tempted to sin. Pray for God's strength and guidance and ask for His forgiveness when you fail. Record your experiences in your journal. Thank God for His love and forgiveness.

Additional Bible readings for this week: Psalms 86 and 130; and Isaiah 53. Copy and attach to a mirror or other place you see daily the words of Psalm 130:7.

Use the prayer starters each day as you come to the Lord in your quiet time, either writing in your own endings or leaving the lines blank to be used in a new way each day.

For next week, reread Psalms 38 and 51. Read through Session 4, filling in any responses as you like.

Journal Page

_____

_____

_____

_____

_____

_____

_____

_____

_____

_____

_____

_____

_____

_____

_____

_____

_____

_____

_____

_____

_____

_____

_____

_____

_____

_____

_____

_____

_____

_____

O Lord, You are so _____

_____

_____

and I am so _____ :

_____

_____

_____

Please forgive me for _____ :

_____

_____

_____

Help me _____

_____

_____

_____

Please bless and take care of _____

_____

_____

_____

Thanks, Lord, for _____

_____

_____

_____

Session 4
God's Assuring Love

Where Are We Going?

We will take a deeper look at Psalm 51 to discover
the love God has ready to pour out on us for the sake of
Jesus, as we turn to Him in repentance and contrition,
confessing our sins and acknowledging our need of Him.

Ready, Set, Go

Begin with prayer. Thank God for the study of His
Word, for showing you not only your sin and its conse-
quences but also that He has provided a way back to
Him.

Spend a few minutes on "**Where Am I Now?**" to
determine which things are movable by your own
strength. Get into "**The Search,**" digging into the psalm
to discover God's rich grace and love for you.

Take time to "**Respond**" as you praise God for the
renewal of your life and the re-created heart He gives
you. Pray together in praise to God for all He does and
has done for you.

Before the next session, do the "**Do,**" recording your
thoughts and experiences in the journal page following
this session, filling in the prayer page or using it as a
way to pray each day.

Where Am I Now?

Listed below are items that need to be lifted or
moved. Using a scale from 1 to 10, with 1 representing
the least amount of strength needed to lift or move and
10 the most, write in the number that best describes

your strength. If you have no strength at all to move
something, write in 0.

___ Piano	___ Pencil
___ Box of books	___ Hammer
___ Computer	___ Greed
___ Mixing bowl	___ Pride
___ Vase of flowers	___ Unhappiness
___ A two-year-old	___ Jealousy
___ Basket of clothes	___ Sin

The Search

Sin Brings Guilt

Psalm 51 is a psalm written by David after the
prophet Nathan confronted him with his sins—adultery
with Bathsheba and ordering that Uriah be killed.

1a. Review 2 Samuel 12:1–13. Describe the task that
God gave Nathan. Why might that have been difficult
for him? Why was it necessary?

1b. Why is it difficult to confront a family member
or friend with the truth about his or her sin? to be confronted by someone about our own sin? Why is it necessary? Why might what is said make a difference in that
person's life? in that person's eternal salvation?

Psalm 51 is David's confession to God of his fall.
Having been condemned by Nathan the prophet, David
saw the enormity and atrociousness of his sin and realized that he had rebelled against God and broken His
commandment. The psalm begins with David throwing
himself on God's mercy, knowing he had no excuse, no
just argument for his sin. Read verses 1–6.

2a. How does the psalmist describe his sinful condition? List the people David, Eve, and Miriam had sinned against.

2b. Reread verse 4. Whom were their offenses really against?

2c. List here or name to yourself people whom you have sinned against. Then read again Psalm 51:4. Whom is your offense really against? Why is it important to know and acknowledge that?

3a. List the attributes of God that David mentions in Psalm 51:1–6 and compare them to David's list of his own sinfulness. Why does David not remind God of all the good he (David) has done for God's kingdom?

3b. What could Eve and Miriam have said in their own defense or to justify themselves when God confronted them with their sin? Why would their pleas have been in vain?

3c. How have you tried to justify yourself when you realized your sin against God? Why doesn't self-justification work?

Guilt Calls for Repentance

In verse 5 of Psalm 51, David admits not only the guilt from his actual sins of adultery and murder but also declares his sinful condition from the moment of conception. Original sin, that dreadful condition into which

every human being, with the exception of Jesus, is born, is our inheritance from Adam and Eve.

4a. Read verses 7–12. At the time of the Passover, people dipped hyssop (a plant with bitter, pungent leaves) in lamb's blood and spread the blood on the doorposts of their house. Hyssop was also used in the ritual cleansing of those with bruises or skin diseases. Why do you think the psalmist used hyssop to describe the cleansing that he needed? How thorough was the cleansing God gave David, Eve, and Miriam?

4b. How thorough is the cleansing God gives you? Does He leave any part of you unclean? Why is His cleansing complete?

5. Reading these verses, we too can know that we can throw ourselves on the mercy of God, confessing our sins against Him. Ultimately, He is the one we must answer to, for any sin that we commit separates us from Him. To what words of confession from these verses can you relate? Write your own confession of sin.

God Provides Relief

6a. The psalmist desires a number of things from God in verses 7–12, including re-creation. The verb used for "create" is one used only in connection with God and the one used in Genesis 1:1. How did David need to be re-created? Eve? Miriam?

6b. What do you desire of God? How does God offer Himself to you? Think of His Word and Sacraments. How do these renew you?

Respond

In verses 13–19, the psalmist gives his response to God's cleansing mercy. David has relied on God's promise to save, not knowing the full story of the Son who would come from his seed. We have the advantage there over David. We have seen the fulfillment of God's promise of a Savior in the life, death, and resurrection of Jesus. Through His cleansing blood, we are re-created for a new life.

Read verses 13–19, choosing what your response to God's gracious love and mercy will be this week. Take a moment to pray silently about your choice, then share with the rest of the group what you will do.

Finally, pray together, asking God to renew your spirit, to re-create you anew for service and praise to Him.

Do

This week record times in your journal that reveal how God is renewing a right spirit and re-created heart within you. Praise God for His overwhelming love and mercy. Tell someone (Psalm 51:13) what God has done for you.

Additional Bible readings for this week: Isaiah 43:15–21; 44:1–4; Lamentations 3:22–26; and 2 Corinthians 5. Copy and attach to a mirror or other place you see daily the words of Romans 8:1–2.

In your prayers this week, give your broken and contrite heart to God. Write in your own endings to the sentences or leave them blank to be used in a new way each day.

Continue regular Bible reading, prayer, journaling, and worship in your walk with God as He continues to fill you with new life and to re-create your heart.